Election Essentials with the Supervisor of Elections

A Guide to Civics for Young Citizens

Written by Alisa L. Grace

Illustrations by naqsa_art

This Book is Dedicated to:

To our future voters, we desire that children learn about civics and the voting process in a fun and engaging manner. We are committed to engaging them in learning about civics and the vital role of all parties involved in ensuring the success of our voting process.

Dear Parents and Teachers,

We are excited to introduce this new book designed to inspire young minds and foster a deeper understanding of our democratic process. "Elections Essentials with the Supervisor of Elections: A Guide to Civics for Young Citizens" students aged 10-13.

Why Civics Education Matters?

Civics education at an early age plays a crucial role in shaping informed and engaged citizens. By introducing concepts like elections, government branches, and citizens' rights and responsibilities, we equip our students with the tools they need to participate actively in their communities and contribute to the future of our nation.

About the Book

"Elections Essentials with the Supervisor of Elections" provides an engaging and accessible introduction to civics, making complex concepts easy to understand. Through relatable examples and clear explanations, students will gain a foundational understanding of the election process and their role in it.

What to Expect

Students will:

- Gain a foundational understanding of the election process.
- Explore the roles and functions of different levels of government.
- Develop an appreciation for the rights and freedoms guaranteed by our Constitution.
- Learn how to make informed decisions and express their opinions thoughtfully.

Family Engagement

We encourage you to discuss these civics concepts with your child at home. Ask them about what they're learning, explore related topics together, and model active citizenship in your own lives.

Together, we can empower the next generation to become informed, engaged, and responsible participants in our democratic society.

Sincerely,
Alisa L. Grace

Chapter 1

The Role of the Supervisor of Elections.

"Meet the Supervisor of Elections"

The Supervisor of Elections is a very important person who ensures everything runs smoothly during elections. A supervisor is in charge of a task or group of people. This person oversees or watches all the election activities, ensuring everything is done correctly and fairly. The supervisor handles the administration, which means they oversee all the organizing and managing needed to make an election happen. This includes setting up voting locations, training poll workers, and counting the votes. Having fair and organized elections would be easier with the Supervisor of Elections!

Supervisor of Elections
Register & Vote

Chapter 2

Key Departments and Their Roles

"Why Do Elections Matter?"

Elections are super important because they are a big part of our democracy. A democracy is a type of government where people have the power to make decisions about how the country is run. During an election, citizens (anyone who lives in a country and has the right to vote) get to choose their leaders by voting. These leaders make decisions that affect our schools, parks, and even the rules we follow every day. So, when citizens vote in elections, they help decide what happens in their community and country, ensuring everyone's voice can be heard!

ELECTIONS

A man without a vote is a man without protection.

Chapter 3

The Voting Process

Getting Registered: The Voter Registration Department

The Voter Registration Department helps people get ready to vote by signing them up through registration. Registration means officially adding your name to a list of people who can vote. It's essential because it ensures that only people who meet the requirements or eligibility can vote. Eligibility means you are allowed to do something, like voting, because you meet specific rules, like being a certain age or living in a particular place. Once you register, your name is added to an extensive database, like a giant computer list that keeps track of all the voters. This way, the Voter Registration Department ensures everyone eligible can have their voice heard in elections.

vote

"Spreading the Word: The Outreach Department"

The Outreach Department is like the cheerleaders of the election world, ensuring everyone knows how important voting is. Outreach means reaching out to people to share information and help them get involved. This department works hard to engage, connect with the community, and get people excited about voting. They do this through education, teaching people about the voting process and its importance. By spreading the word, the Outreach Department helps ensure that as many people as possible participate in elections and have their voices heard.

ELECTION

"Behind the Machines: The Election Equipment Department"

The Election Equipment Department takes care of all the cool gadgets used during elections to ensure voting is easy and accurate. A critical piece of equipment is the scanner, which reads and counts votes on the ballots. Some places use electronic voting, where you vote on a computer instead of paper. These machines are super important because they help ensure every vote is counted correctly and we get accurate results from the election.

EVERY
VOTE
COUNTS

"Election Day Helpers: The Poll Worker Department"

On Election Day, poll workers are excellent helpers who ensure everything goes smoothly at the voting places. A poll worker is a person who helps manage the voting process at a polling place, which is a specific location where people can go to vote. Poll workers have many duties, like checking in voters, giving them ballots, and helping them understand how to vote if they need assistance. Assistance means giving help or support to someone. By doing their jobs well, poll workers ensure everyone has a fair and accessible time voting on Election Day!

"From Registration to Casting a Vote"

Voting is an exciting process, and here's a step-by-step guide to help you understand it. First, you must register to vote, which means signing up to be on the list of people allowed to vote. Once you're registered, you'll need to find your polling place, which is the location where you go to vote. On Election Day, you'll go to your polling place and bring your valid photo and signature ID to prove who you are. You'll receive a ballot to mark your choices when you're there. Finally, you cast your vote by putting your ballot into a machine that counts it. This process helps ensure everyone's voice is heard in the election!

STEP-01
REGISTER TO VOTE

STEP-02
POLLING PLACE

STEP-03
VOTER ID

STEP-04
CASTING YOUR VOTE

Chapter 4

Counting the Votes

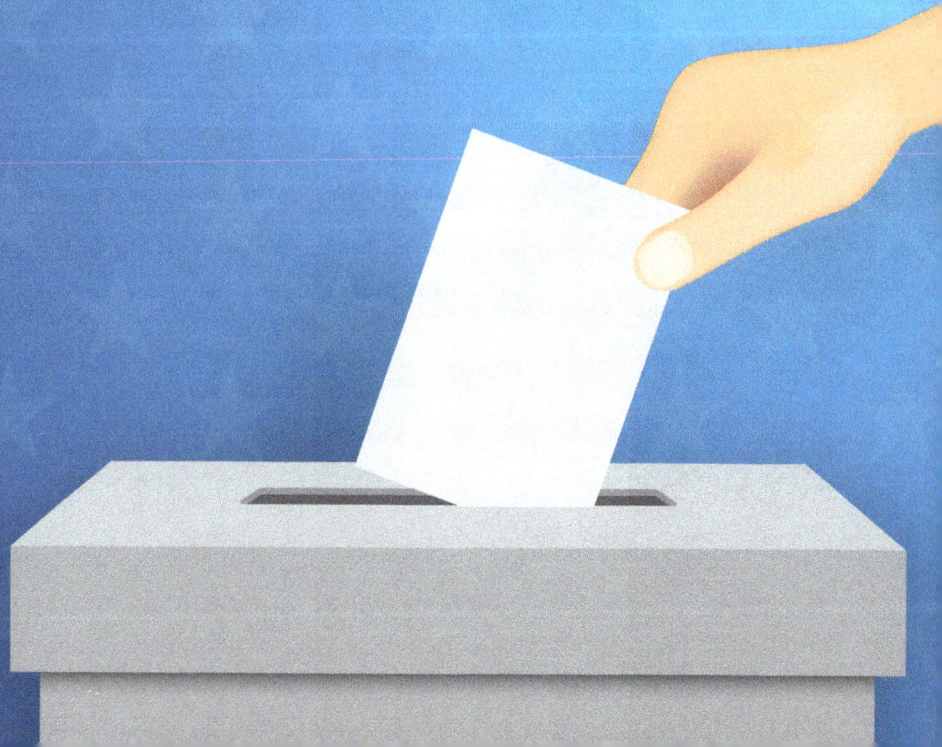

"How Votes Are Counted"

After everyone has marked their ballots, they put the ballot in a scanner to count or tabulate their votes accurately. Accuracy, which means being correct and without mistakes, is super important because it ensures that the true winners are chosen. Another crucial part of counting votes is transparency, which means the process is open and transparent for everyone. This way, people can trust that the election is fair and honest.

Chapter 5

Why Voting Matters

"The Impact of Your Vote"

Your vote is powerful and can significantly impact your community, state, and country. Impact means the strong effect something has. When you vote, you help choose leaders who make crucial decisions. These decisions can become laws, known as legislation, that affect everything from schools to the environment. Voting also ensures that you have representation, meaning people in government who speak up for your needs and ideas. For example, elections have led to significant changes like new parks, better roads, and laws protecting animals. So, when you vote, you help shape the future!

Conclusion

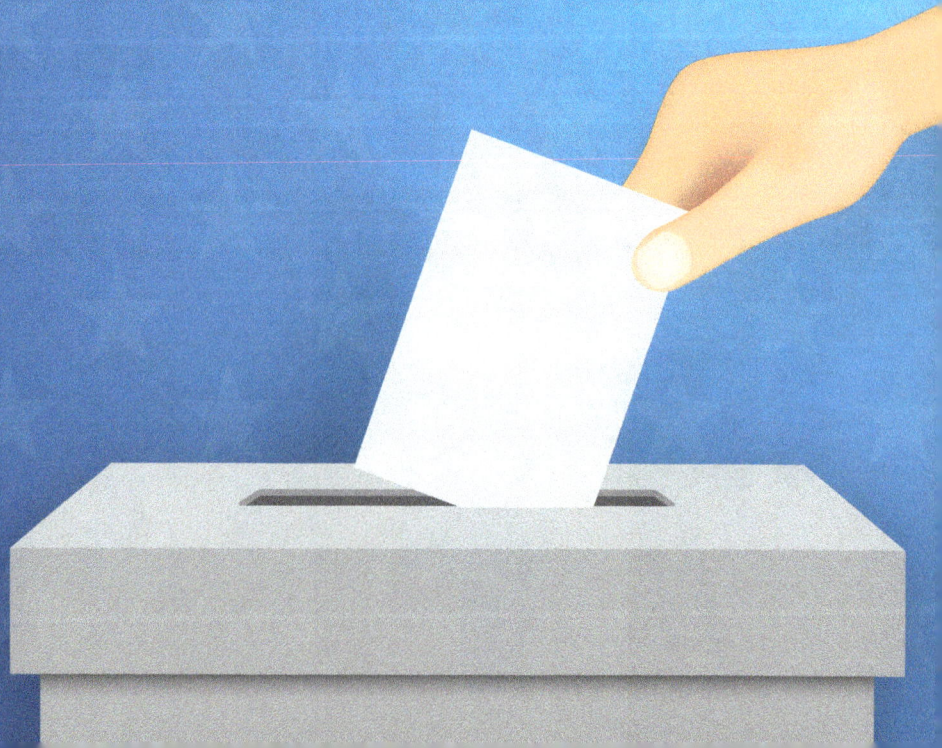

"Becoming an Active Citizen"

Even if you are not old enough to vote, many ways exist to be an active citizen! You can get involved by joining school clubs, helping with local clean-up projects, or attending community events. Doing these things teaches you more about how your community works and how you can make a difference. Plus, when you turn 18, you'll be ready and excited to vote and have your voice heard. Being an active citizen helps make your community a better place for everyone!

"I alone cannot change the world, but I can cast a stone across the waters to create many ripples."

– Mother Teresa

Glossary

Civic Vocabulary

Accuracy: Being correct and without mistakes. In elections, it means counting votes correctly to reflect actual results.

Administration: Organizing and managing tasks. Elections include setting up voting locations and training workers.

Assistance: Giving help or support to someone.

Ballot: The paper or electronic form where voters mark their choices.

Citizen: A person who lives in a country and has the rights and responsibilities of that country.

Democracy: A type of government where people have the power to make decisions through voting.

Election: The process where citizens vote to choose their leaders or decide on laws.

Eligibility: Meeting the requirements to do something, like voting, because of age or residency.

Engagement: Connecting with the community and getting people excited about voting or other activities.

Electronic Voting: Using a computer or machine to vote instead of paper ballots.

Impact: The strong effect something has. Voting can impact laws and decisions.

Legislation: Laws made by the government.

Outreach: Reaching out to people to share information and help them get involved.

Polling Place: The location where people go to vote.

Poll Worker: A person who helps manage the voting process at a polling place.

Precinct: A specific location where people go to vote.

Voter Registration: Voter officially signing up to be on the list of people allowed to vote.

Representation: Having people in government who speak up for your needs and ideas.

Scanner: A machine that reads and counts votes.

Supervisor: Someone in charge of a task or group of people.

Tabulation: The process of counting votes.

Transparency: an open process that is easily visible to everyone, ensuring fairness.

Photo and Signature ID: A particular card or document proving who you are when you vote.

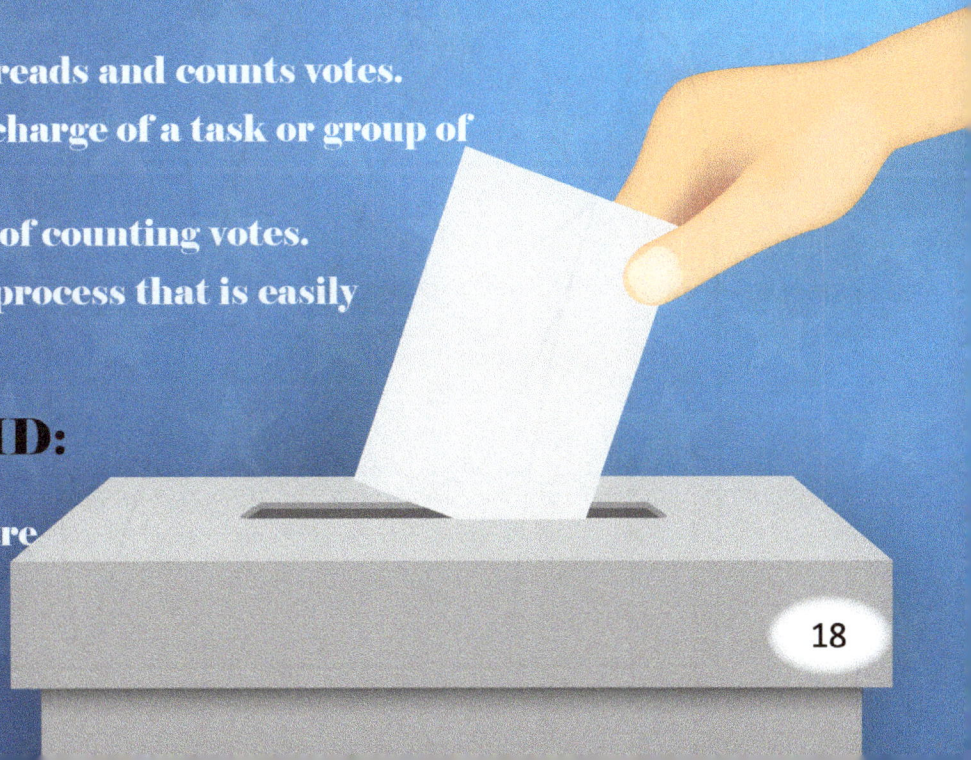

The Supervisor of Elections

WELCOME, FUTURE VOTERS!

REGISTER TO VOTE

Start

End

21

ELECTION DAY HELPERS

```
C  P  R  S  T  A  T  I  O  N
H  R  D  L  P  V  N  X  L  S
E  E  V  T  O  F  L  B  B  X
C  C  N  B  A  L  L  O  T  C
K  I  B  V  L  I  I  L  R  W
I  N  E  H  C  D  H  I  D  O
N  C  A  V  R  H  M  O  E  R
L  T  N  O  I  T  A  T  S  K
A  S  S  I  S  T  A  N  C  E
P  O  L  L  W  O  R  K  E  R
```

Poll worker	Assistance	ID
Precinct	Check in	Station
	Ballot	

WHY VOTING MATTERS

decisions	voice
community	future

1) Empowering connections for a vibrant

   _____

2) _____ shape our path forward

3) Building a brighter _____ together

4) Your _____ matters

(Answers 1. community, 2. decisions, 3. future, 4. voice)

BECOME A CIVIC HERO!

Design Your Own Superhero

DID YOU KNOW
Fun Facts About Elections and Voting:

1) What is the process called where citizens choose their leaders or decide on laws by voting?

2) What type of government allows people to have the power to make decisions through voting?

3) Who is responsible for organizing and overseeing all election activities?

4) What is the piece of paper or electronic form where voters mark their choices called?

5) What do we call a person who helps manage the voting process at a polling place?

6) What must you show at a polling place to prove who you are before you can vote?

7) What is the name of the machine that reads and counts votes?

8) What is it called when counting votes is done correctly and without mistakes?

9) What is the unique list where all the registered voters' names are kept?

10) What do we call the process of counting votes?

ASSISTING VOTERS

THANKS FOR LEARNING WITH US!

Thank You Voters

Voted!

Voted!
Election Day

Voted!
Election Day

Meet the Author

Meet Alisa Ladawn Grace, a retired school administrator, Chief Operating Officer of a nonprofit company, Transformation Life Coach, and a fervent advocate for children's civic education. Alisa has authored not one but three engaging and informative children's books focused on civics: "Civic Heroes: Discovering Elections with the Supervisor of Elections" (ages 6-9), "My Civic Adventure: Learning About Voting and Community!" (ages 3-5), and "Election Essentials with the Supervisor of Elections: A Guide to Civics for Young Citizens" (ages 10-13).

Recognizing the importance of early civic education, Alisa's books introduce children to fundamental concepts like democracy, voting rights, and the electoral process in an age-appropriate and enjoyable way. Her work aims to inspire the next generation of informed and responsible voters, empowering them to participate in their communities and actively shape a better future.

Alisa's belief in the potential of young minds is deeply rooted in her diverse experiences. From her career in education to her role as a Transformation Life Coach, she has seen firsthand the transformative power of guidance. Her passion for guiding individuals toward personal growth and spiritual fulfillment is a belief and a mission evident in her writing.writing.

Alisa's practical guide, "Unlocking Your Great Potential Within You: The Supernatural Powers of Meditation, Executive Functioning Skills, and Good Habits for Kids 3-18 Years Old," Is not just a book but a toolkit for success and well-being. It equips children with tools they can apply immediately, emphasizing the importance of faith, integrity, and love in an immediately applicable way.

Through her writing, Alisa seeks to make a positive difference in the lives of children and families, fostering a lifelong commitment to civic engagement and unlocking the great potential of every young citizen.

www.ingramcontent.com/pod-product-compliance
Lightning Source LLC
LaVergne TN
LVHW061331060426
835513LV00015B/1358